EXOTIC
PETS
FROM ALLIGATORS
TO ZEBRA FISH

EXOTIC PETS

FROM ALLIGATORS TO ZEBRA FISH

John Zeaman

Before They Were Pets

FRANKLIN WATTS
New York London Hong Kong Sydney
Danbury, Connecticut

Cover and interior design by Robin Hoffmann/Brand X Studios
Illustrations by Steve Savage

Photographs ©: Animals Animals: 43 (Richard Shiell), cover top right (Renee Stockdale); Art Resource: 54; BBC Natural History Unit: 37 (Mary Ann McDonald), 30, 31 (Colin Seddon), 16 (Artur Tabor); Bob Shanley: 46; Gamma-Liaison: 49 (Paul S. Howell), 39 (Keister), 41 (Alfonso Mejia), 36 (P. Wallet); Lynn M. Stone: 18 right, 18 left; Peter Arnold Inc.: 2 (John Cancalosi); Photo Researchers: cover bottom left, 9 (Tom McHugh), 8 (Jany Sauvane), 28 (Dan Suzio); Ron Norman: cover center; Superstock, Inc.: cover top left, cover bottom right, 21, 24, 25, 51; The Gorilla Foundation: 19 (Dr. Ronald H. Cohen); Tony Stone Images: 6 (Elie Bernager), 10 (Gay Bumgarner), 14, 42 (Myrleen Cate), 35 (Tim Flach), 53 (Rich Frishman), 20 (Hulton Getty), 48 (Rodale Stock), 13 (David Woodfall); Wildlife Collection: 15 (Gary Schultz), 29 (Tom Vezo), 45 (Staffan Widstrand).

Visit Franklin Watts on the Internet at:
http://publishing.grolier.com

Library of Congress Cataloging-in-Publication Data
Zeaman, John.
Exotic pets: from alligators to zebra fish / John Zeaman.
p. cm. — (Before they were pets)
Includes bibliographical references and index.
Summary: Discusses the practice which people throughout history and around the world have had for choosing pets from among an enormous variety of wild animals.
ISBN 0-531-20352-2 (lib. bdg.)   0-531-15949-3 (pbk.)
1. Wild animals as pets—Juvenile literature.   [1. Wild animals as pets.]
I. Title.   II. Series: Zeaman, John. Before they were pets.
SF416.2.Z4   1999
636.088'7—dc21   97-50144
                                                               CIP
                                                               AC

GROLIER
PUBLISHING

CONTENTS

This boy is excited about his first pet—a goldfish.

INTRODUCTION

We share this planet with an incredible variety of animals. But, out of many thousands of **species**, only a few have achieved the special status of pets. And an even smaller number have become true animal companions.

People are continually striving to expand the number of animals we call pets. There is hardly an animal on Earth that someone hasn't tried to tame or keep. Throughout history, kings and emperors have kept animals as pets. Native Americans and other tribal people have tamed moose, jaguars, and even giant eels! Movie stars and other wealthy people sometimes keep exotic and dangerous animals, such as leopards or ocelots. It is no longer unusual

Snake Charmers

Snakes were first kept as pets by snake charmers in Africa and Asia. These people play music and fascinate snakes with movements. The snakes respond by swaying back and forth, as if in response to the music.

A man exercising his pet boa constrictor

to hear that someone keeps a boa constrictor, a skunk, or a tarantula.

When people keep an animal that is not normally tamed or kept as a companion, it is called an **exotic** pet. The word *exotic* means "special" or "unusual." A leopard, of course, would be an exotic pet—so would a rattlesnake. Some animals, such as ferrets or miniature pigs, were once considered exotic pets, but today, they are fairly common.

WHY AN EXOTIC PET?

Why do people want to keep unusual animals? What makes humans want to turn wild, and sometimes dangerous, creatures into pets? The desire to have an unusual pet probably is no different from the desire to have anything unusual—an antique car, a rare stamp, or an expensive toy, for instance. Many people own dogs or cats, but how many own a hedgehog? Having an exotic pet can also be more interesting and adventurous than having an ordinary pet.

This young man enjoys having his picture taken with his pet hedgehog.

This woman is caring for an orphaned raccoon.

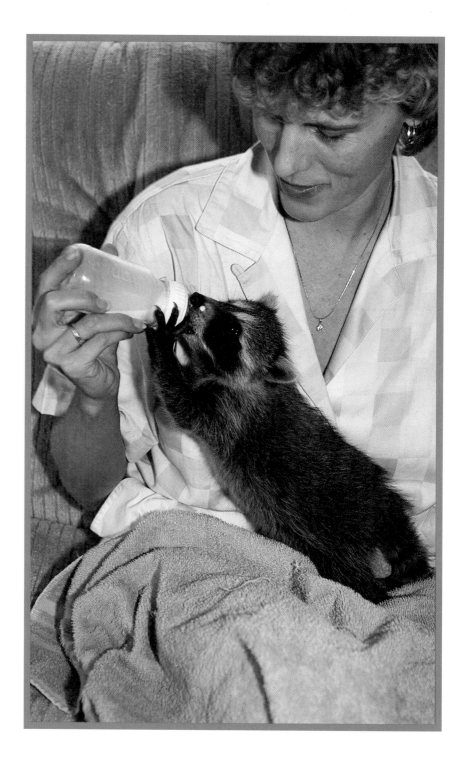

In addition, human beings have a strong, deeply rooted desire to tame wild creatures. There is something inherently satisfying about bridging the gap of fear and caution that separates us from so much of the animal kingdom. Anyone who nurses a fledgling bird or raises a baby raccoon knows the special rewards of bringing a creature in from the wild and making it friendly.

The practice of keeping exotic pets tells us a lot about ourselves and what we want and expect from other creatures. At the same time, it tells us something about the animals. Not every effort to tame a wild creature is successful. Not every animal makes a "good" pet. And yet, we are fascinated when we hear stories about people who tame coyotes or bears, or keep an owl in the house.

Moose as Pets

In the 1700s, a traveler to North America reported seeing moose that were as tame as sheep. When Native Americans traveled by canoe, the moose often walked along the shore, following their masters. At night, when the people camped, the moose stayed close to the tents.

CHAPTER 1

CAN ANY ANIMAL BE A PET?

What does it mean to call an animal a pet? If you found a toad outside, brought it into your home, and put it in a tank, would that make it a pet? You would feed it like a pet. You would probably take it out and hold it in your hands from time to time. You might even bring it out in the backyard for a little recreation.

Your toad would certainly be a pet in the same way that many animals purchased at pet stores are pets. The behavior of pet-store goldfish, lizards, or snakes is little different from that of a wild toad.

But these animals are not pets in the same way as a dog or a cat. Dogs and cats are true animal companions.

Three girls looking at a common toad

They are not kept in cages. They usually know their names, come when they are called, and show affection for us. Compared to these animals, the toad or the fish is a captive. If you give the toad an opportunity to escape, it will hop away to freedom without giving you a second thought.

It's important to distinguish between animals that are truly tame and those that are only captives. A true pet isn't just an animal that you have tied up or put in a cage. To

Dogs are true companion animals. This puppy is showing affection for its owner.

be a true pet, rather than a captive, an animal must give up some of its wildness and undergo some changes.

Becoming a pet takes a long time—thousands and thousands of years—and involves several stages of **domestication**. Many of the animals we treasure as pets today, started out as **prey**. They probably were first hunted for meat or pelts, then made captives, and then became helpers.

The wolf became the dog in just that way. Wolves were tamed and then bred by people to help them during hunts, guard their homes, and pull their sleds. Eventually, they became the faithful four-legged friends we know today as dogs.

Other animals have also proved their worth—cats catch mice and other pests, horses carry us on their backs, pigeons relay messages, and other birds entertain us with their songs.

The animals that became our closest companions started out by being useful to us in some way. Over thousands of years, domestication has changed them into animals that are very different from their wild ancestors.

Even today, dogs still pull sleds in some parts of the world.

This orphaned red squirrel is being fed with an eyedropper.

DOMESTICATION OCCURS IN THREE STAGES

Certain physical and emotional changes begin to occur as soon as wild animals come under human care. Over several generations, these animals develop smaller teeth and bodies. In many cases, animals that depend on people for food and protection don't mature entirely. Even when they are several years old, they act more like young animals than do their wild counterparts.

A young animal that is fed and handled by a person forms an attachment to that person and learns new behaviors from the person just as it would from its mother. This is how animals become **tamed**. A tame animal is friendlier than a wild one. When carried to its furthest extreme, taming can include training—teaching an animal to obey commands, do tricks, or respond to its name.

Because taming involves learned behavior, it affects only individual animals. A tame animal does not pass on learned behaviors to its young. For example, if you tame a squirrel and that squirrel has babies, the babies will be born wild. They will have to be tamed just as their mother was.

Breeding has more far-reaching effects, however. It involves raising successive generations of animals in order to bring out certain qualities that will make that species more useful or easier to live with. These qualities are passed from parent to child by **genes** located in an animal's cells. Each gene carries information that determines what an animal looks like and, to some extent, how it behaves.

When people started breeding wolves, they wanted to develop animals that were gentle and cooperative, so they chose the wolves with these qualities and bred them with each other. The pups of these wolves tended to be even more gentle and cooperative. The genes the young wolves

17

inherited from their parents determined their behavior. When the young wolves had pups of their own, the babies were even more gentle and cooperative. Breeding is what accounts for all the differences in dogs—their sizes, shapes, and personalities.

To get along well with people, most pets must undergo natural changes as well as a combination of breeding and

A bearded collie (left) and a basset hound (below) look very different. They are just two types of dogs bred by humans.

CAN AN ANIMAL HAVE A PET?

Friendships between different species of animals don't seem to exist in the wild, but animals kept by the same owner often become friends. A dog may view the household's cat as part of its pack and protect it from other dogs or cats. A cat, in turn, may greet a dog as if the dog were its mother.

Koko, a gorilla, that learned sign language from a group of scientists, asked for a pet. The researchers gave Koko a kitten, which she named "All Ball" in sign language. Koko lovingly cared for the kitten. In fact, Koko showed many of the same feelings for the kitten that people show for their pets.

Koko, a lowland gorilla, gently touches her pet kitten for the first time.

19

taming. Horses, for example, have been bred for thousands of years to carry people on their backs, but each horse must still be tamed for riding.

CAN THEY BE PETS?

By now you're probably thinking that almost any animal might be made into a companion pet. Could you start with an alligator and, through taming and breeding, turn it into an affectionate, loyal pet?

In fact, baby alligators have been kept as pets. Young alligators, the size of large lizards, were frequently sold as pets in the 1950s. Of course, as they grew larger, people became concerned. After all, you can't keep a full-grown

Whenever Captain J. Edwards took one of his pet alligators for a spin, he insisted that they buckle up.

alligator in an aquarium—or in any other type of indoor container. They certainly are not affectionate or communicative. In fact, as adults, they are very dangerous. That's why many people got rid of them, usually by flushing them down a toilet. This gave rise to stories of full-grown alligators living in the sewers of large cities, such as New York.

Alligators simply don't have the potential to be animal companions. They are not intelligent enough or friendly enough to be changed either by breeding or taming. People were able to mold cats and dogs into true pets because these animals had some of the necessary qualities to begin with.

There is no simple way to predict which animals will make good pets. Horses, for example, have had a very close relationship with people for thousands of years. But zebras, which are very similar to horses, have never been domesticated.

Still Growing

Reptiles and amphibians continue to grow, slowly but steadily, throughout their lives.

Zebras do not make good pets.

And while the African wildcat is easily tamed, the European wildcat is a nasty animal that does not make a good pet. You might expect that gorillas, which are closely related to us, would have a natural kinship with humans, but they do not. Although some scientists have tamed gorillas—and even taught them sign language—gorillas do not make easy and natural companions.

CHAPTER 2

PETS OF TRIBAL PEOPLE

Why do people keep pets? Some social scientists speculate that people in modern societies keep pets because they feel cut off from nature. Today, most people live in cities or suburban areas where there are few animals. Pets, according to this theory, are a way for modern people to feel closer to the natural world.

Perhaps there is some truth to this explanation. But is it entirely true? What about tribal people, such as Native Americans, who live close to nature and are surrounded by animals? According to the theory, they would have no desire for pets. But, in fact, the opposite is true.

Although tribal people live as close to nature as people can, they generally keep more pets than people in civilized societies. People who live close to nature have more opportunity to tame a large variety of animals and keep them as pets. In the past, Native Americans of North America made pets of raccoons, moose, bison calves, wolves, and even young bears.

The native people of South America had an even greater variety of pets. An English naturalist traveling in the Amazon region in the 1800s discovered that the local tribes had tamed more than twenty-two kinds of four-legged animals. The Guiana, Caraja, and Barasana considered animal-taming a hobby and an art. Visitors reported seeing villages in which parrots and other birds perched on roof poles, while pigs, dogs, cats, and tame

This Kuna woman and her pet toucan live on a small island off the coast of Panama.

25

ducks wandered in and out of the huts through holes in the walls. The women of these tribes also tamed monkeys, deer, ocelots, tapirs, and small rodents. A medicine man from one tribe earned a reputation by taming and keeping a jaguar.

The Polynesians were also very enthusiastic about pets. At one time, people living on the island of Fiji made pets of fruit bats, lizards, and parrots. The people who lived on the island of Samoa kept pet pigeons and eels. According to one visitor, a young Samoan chief kept his pet eels in large holes partially filled with water. The eels surfaced when the young man whistled to them and even ate out of his hand!

From these examples, we see that there is a deep-rooted human need to keep pets. Since the lives of these tribal people are similar to those of our hunter-gatherer ancestors, they can help us understand why our ancestors first kept animals as pets.

CHAPTER 23

ADOPTING WILD ANIMALS

Tribal people are not the only ones who tame wild animals. Many people in modern societies also enjoy taming all kinds of animals. Do you like to look for and capture little animals? Have you ever lifted a rock and found a squirmy salamander? With a little imagination, even an earthworm, a garden snail, a pillbug, or a firefly can be called a pet.

Keeping a tadpole or a caterpillar can give you the opportunity to observe **metamorphosis**—the process by which some young animals become adults. A tadpole

Always a Tadpole

The axolotl is a tadpole that never grows up. It was originally the larval form of a Mexican salamander, but evolved into a creature that remains in the tadpole state for its entire life.

This frog has grown the legs of an adult, but has not yet lost the tail of a tadpole.

grows legs, loses its tail, and becomes a frog, A caterpillar builds a cocoon, wraps itself inside, and turns into a moth or a butterfly. Before you do catch and keep a small animal that lives near your home, talk to a local wildlife officer or a game warden. In the United States, more than 200 animals are on the **endangered** species list. These animals cannot be captured without permission.

You should also remember that raising a wild animal can be dangerous. For example, some birds could scratch you with their sharp beaks or claws. Raccoons, foxes, or otters may bite. In some cases, wild animals carry a disease called **rabies**. Rabid animals often act strangely. Most cases of wildlife rabies are found in skunks, raccoons, foxes, squirrels, and bats. Because of these potential dangers, you should not try to raise a wild animal without the help and advice of a local wildlife officer or game warden.

If you see a raccoon, do not get too close. Many raccoons carry rabies.

Hidden Babies

If the car you are riding in accidentally hits a female opossum in spring or summer, check to see if she has babies with her. Tiny newborns may be found in the pouch on her abdomen, while slightly older babies may be clinging to the fur on her back.

Raising wild animals can be even more difficult in suburban areas or cities. Animals trained by people in rural areas are closer to their natural environment than those raised in a city apartment, for example. You should also follow local rules and laws about keeping wildlife in your home or yard.

ORPHANED AND INJURED ANIMALS

You may know someone who has tamed a squirrel, bird, raccoon, opossum, fox, or even a coyote. In many cases, the wild animal may have become attached to the person because its mother died and it was too small to survive on

This hedgehog came to a wildlife hospital with a broken leg. A veterinarian put a splint on the leg.

its own. Or, the animal may have been injured and the person nursed it back to health.

It is usually best to return an orphaned or injured animal to the wild as soon as it can cope on its own. But some people grow attached to these pets and want to keep them. If you do keep a wild animal, it is important to know all its needs.

A baby animal can be kept in a box filled with soft material. A light bulb should be used to keep the baby warm. Young **mammals** can be fed a mixture of milk and egg yolk. If the animal is very small, the formula should be given through an eyedropper. If the animal is larger use a baby bottle. Baby birds can be fed small pieces of dry cat food soaked in a mixture of egg yolk and milk. A hungry baby bird will **gape**—lift its head and open its mouth

Human Odor

Has anyone ever told you not to touch a baby bird? Many people believe that the mother bird will abandon the baby if it smells your scent on the chick. In most cases, this is not true. Nevertheless, young animals should not be handled because they may get lost or hurt trying to escape.

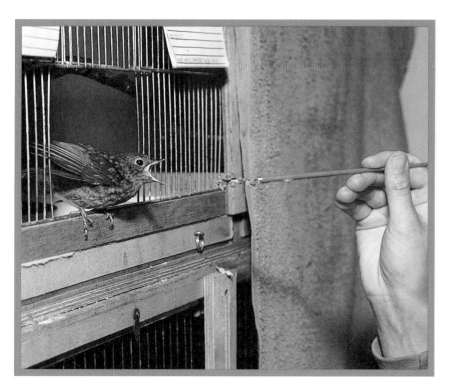

This baby robin was abandoned by its mother. Luckily, some people are now caring for it.

SETTING THEM FREE

After being kept as a pet, some animals can easily adapt to life in the wild, while others cannot. A raccoon or a squirrel can be returned to its native habitat if it is given a short transitional period. The transition might involve keeping the cage outside with the door open. This allows the animal to come and go as it pleases.

Snakes, opossums, and turtles are examples of animals that can be released without a transitional period. Animals that have been altered in any way—by declawing, de-scenting, or neutering—should never be set free. They will not be able to survive in the wild.

wide—for food. When it gapes, a pea-sized pellet of food can be poked down its throat.

A frog needs a **vivarium**—a tank that has both land and water areas in it. Because a frog breathes through its skin as well as through its lungs, it must live in a moist environment. Frogs eat live food, so you must either catch insects for them or buy live crickets or mealworms (the larvae of beetles) from a pet store. You could also try jiggling a small piece of meat in front of the frog, to make it think the food is alive.

Some caterpillars eat only the leaves of a certain plant, such as milkweed or apple trees. Your pet caterpillar will die unless you provide the right food. Some turtles will only swallow their food underwater.

Sometimes people release an animal into the wild after it has been a pet for a long time. This is not always a good idea. A famous book called *The Yearling* tells the story of a boy who tries to raise a young deer. The story has a sad ending because the deer's behavior makes it unsuitable for life on a farm. This book contains an important lesson—taming a wild animal can upset the natural order of things.

CHAPTER 4

EXOTIC PETS: A CLOSER LOOK

FISH AS PETS

Many people keep fish because they enjoy watching them and learning about their behavior. Although some kinds of tropical fish have been bred in a variety of shapes and sizes, they are not true pets because their behavior has not changed. Fish may respond to us in some ways, such as when we feed them, but they remain basically unchanged from their wild counterparts.

The most unusual type of pet fish is a kind of carp called the koi. These brightly colored fish are about 36

A koi fish is about to catch its dinner—a goldfish.

inches (91 cm) long and live up to 40 years. Because they are so large, koi require an outdoor pond. These fish are valued for their unusual colors, which are produced by pigments located beneath the scales.

BIG CATS AND OTHER PREDATORS

Joy Adamson's book *Born Free* tells how she befriended and tamed lions in Africa. It demonstrates that even the most fierce and dangerous cats can form close attachments to people. It's important to remember, however, that these animals were not taken out of their natural environment. Keeping a lion as a house pet would be cruel to the animal and difficult for the owner.

Nevertheless, some people keep large cats as pets. In most cases, they do it because they want to be noticed. A

Expensive Fish

The Japanese refer to the beautifully colored koi as "living jewels." Koi with unusual color patterns can sell for hundreds of thousands of dollars.

Siegfried and Roy are famous magicians. They often use large cats in their act.

movie star with a pet leopard or a shaman with a tame jaguar are trying to get attention and admiration from other people. Keeping a "dangerous" animal implies that the owner is a powerful person. Cheetahs, the fastest mammals in the world, were kept as pets by rulers in ancient Egypt. More recently, they were kept by people living in North Africa. The owners valued these animals for their exotic appearance and good behavior. In some cases, the cheetahs were used as hunting companions. If it

has been raised properly, a full-grown cheetah remains responsive to people.

The elegant and relatively small ocelot was once a favorite pet among rich and eccentric people. Ocelots can be affectionate animals, and a few are still kept as pets. Today, cheetahs and ocelots, as well as tigers, jaguars, and leopards, are all endangered. It is illegal to buy them or to keep them as pets.

The North American mountain lion, also called the cougar or puma, has recently gained popularity as a pet in the western United States. (It is endangered in the eastern United States.) Because these cats are perceived as dangerous, their owners boast about their success in taming

A man with his pet mountain lion

THE MYSTERIOUS MAPACH

In the 1500s, a Spanish explorer named Francisco Hernandez noticed an unfamiliar animal living in the homes of Native Americans in Mexico. He described the animal, which the people called a "mapach," as the size of a small dog with a large head, small ears, a doglike muzzle, white stripes, a long tail, and ". . . humanlike feet and hands with which it appears to feel everything."

Hernandez also said that this animal ". . . is constantly pestering people it knows and will follow them with great affection. It lies next to them and rolls around happily in the soil, amusing itself and gamboling in a thousand different ways."

What was this strange, friendly animal? Judging by the description and the accompanying illustration, the "mapach" was none other than the animal we know as the raccoon.

and keeping them. Like other wild cats, they are easiest to keep when they are young. Adults cannot stay indoors once they are full grown.

Young raccoons are affectionate and playful. They make delightful pets. Adult raccoons are a different story. They are too destructive to be allowed the run of a house. At the same time, they are too bright and active to be shut up in a cage. The raccoon's cousin, the kinkajou, is a much more agreeable pet. This creature, which is often called the honey bear, looks more like a monkey than a raccoon. Although kinkajous were once fairly popular pets, they are now relatively rare and, as a result, difficult to find.

SPIDERS AND SCORPIONS

Although very few kinds of spiders are dangerous, many people fear them. Some spiders—especially those that spin webs—are interesting to watch. And although tarantulas have a bad reputation, the kind found in the United States is actually no more dangerous than a bee or a wasp. Because tarantulas are larger than most spiders, they would rather feed on small mice than on flying insects and can kill prey with surprising speed and efficiency.

A girl with her pet tarantula

39

The scorpion is one of the oldest animals on Earth. Although some species are poisonous, most American scorpions are not. Many of the scorpions sold in pet stores are African or Malaysian. They look very threatening and can give you a painful nip with their claws.

SNAKES AND LIZARDS

Another pet that makes many people uncomfortable is the snake. In fact, even our close relatives—the monkeys—are instinctively afraid of snakes.

Some people, however, are fascinated by snakes and enjoy keeping them as pets. Snakes are actually fairly easy to care for. Over time, they grow accustomed to being handled, and some even seem to enjoy the warmth of the human touch. The biggest problem with having a pet snake is keeping it. Because snakes can slip through the tiniest crack or space, they often escape from their cages and slither into a dark corner.

The large boa, or python, which kills its prey by squeezing it, is a fairly popular pet. The common boa, or boa constrictor, can be up to 10 feet (3 m) long, while the reticulated python can grow to a size of 26 feet (8 m). These snakes can be dangerous, especially around small children. Smaller boas or pythons tend to make better pets. Many of them are only about 36 inches (91 cm) long.

Snakes belong to a group of animals called **reptiles**. All reptiles are **cold blooded**—their body temperature varies with the temperature of their surroundings. Snake owners who live in colder regions of the world must use a spotlight or heater to warm their pet's home. Most snakes eat mice or rabbits.

False Scent

Snakes prefer to eat animals they have killed themselves. However, it is possible to trick a snake by marking meat with the scent of a live mouse or toad.

Baby Turtle Ban

At one time, millions of baby turtles were sold as pets every year. But in 1975, scientists discovered that many of the turtles were carriers of a dangerous bacteria called salmonella. As a result, the sale of turtles less than 4 inches (10 cm) in diameter was banned in the United States.

This boy takes his pet boa constrictor everywhere he goes.

Lizards, another kind of reptile, are also kept as pets. In Asia, house geckos often live inside people's homes. The people do not mind because the geckos crawl about on the walls catching insects. In North America, some people keep iguanas—friendly lizards that respond well to handling and grow to be quite tame. Many owners occasionally carry their iguanas around or let them run freely about the house. Some adult iguanas are 6 feet (1.8 m) long. Obviously, they must be kept in a large enclosure.

This iguana likes to hang out on its owner's head.

CAN INSECTS BE PETS?

Because each ant has a certain role in its community, they are fascinating to watch. Many toy stores sell ant farms in transparent plastic containers so that you can observe the ants as they build tunnels, store food, and lay eggs.

The praying mantis makes an interesting pet. It responds to people more than most other insects. The praying mantis gets its name from its hunting position—front legs folded, body bent forward. It catches its prey with its pincerlike front legs.

Insect Thermometers

Crickets tend to sing faster in warm weather. In fact, some scientists can predict the air temperature by counting the number of chirps made by one cricket over a certain period of time.

A praying mantis makes an interesting pet.

The mantis can move its head from side to side, so if you keep one in a cage, it is easy to feed the insect. If you handle a praying mantis every day, it becomes accustomed to sitting on your finger as you feed it.

Crickets were probably the first insect kept as pets. In ancient times, the Chinese kept crickets in elaborate wooden cages. They appreciated the fighting prowess of crickets as well as the musical sounds they make with their wings. The Chinese believed that crickets brought good luck.

MONKEYS AS PETS

Monkeys are a lot like us, so you might think they would make good pets. For centuries, they have been kept by all sorts of people—from royalty to street-strolling organ-grinders.

In recent years, many people have kept spider monkeys, marmosets, squirrel monkeys, and woolly monkeys as pets. Although they can be entertaining to watch, most people find them difficult to handle and they do not make good pets. Monkeys are often aggressive and excitable, and they are very messy eaters. Also, despite their intelligence, monkeys are almost impossible to housebreak. If they are kept in the house, they must wear diapers.

PET FADS

Several years ago, skunks were a popular exotic pet. Few are available today, however, because even de-scented skunks are difficult to keep. Skunks sleep a lot, especially in winter, and can be troublesome when they are awake. If they are confined for long periods, they may become aggressive. In some cases, they bite and scratch their owners.

Warring Ants

If you keep ants, make sure they all come from the same colony. Ants from different colonies will wage war against one another. Some ants will even capture and make slaves of ants from other colonies.

A girl with her capuchin monkey

A man gives his pet pot-bellied pig a treat.

In recent years, African pygmy hedgehogs have become increasingly popular. They are cute, but their prickly spines make them difficult to pet. In addition, they are solitary and most active at night. As a result, they are not particularly responsive to humans.

The "hot" pet right now is the miniature potbellied pig. These pigs, which were first bred in Vietnam and China, were introduced into the United States and Canada in 1985. Since then, they have become very popular.

They are smart, responsive, affectionate and are easier to train than cats or horses. In fact, the average miniature potbellied pig is not much more difficult to keep than a dog. As adults, they weigh about 100 pounds (45 kg) and are about 18 inches (46 cm) in length.

CHAPTER 25

THE HUMAN-ANIMAL BOND

A CONTRACT WITH PETS

In becoming pets, animals sacrifice their freedom. Most of the time, horses are kept in small corrals and exercised only when their owner wants a ride. Dogs and potbellied pigs must learn to walk on a leash. They live in fenced yards or even in high-rise apartment buildings. Lizards, snakes, insects, and spiders are usually confined to small cages. In exchange, however, the animals receive shelter, food, and affection.

More than Pets

Many studies have shown how close people are to their pets. A survey conducted in 1988 found that 95 percent of pet owners thought of their pets as "friends."

Pets provide friendship and companionship.

What do people get from pets? Very simply, pets make our lives more worthwhile. They provide friendship and companionship. They give us something to care for, the way a mother cares for a child. Some pets also do jobs for us and protect us. We can play with most of them, and those we can't play with are usually fun to watch.

We often treat our pets like people. We give them names, and talk to them. We take them to the doctor when they're sick. We hug them, and even let them lick our faces. We treat them like members of our family.

WHEN THINGS GO WRONG

Despite the universal human need to feel close to animals, the bond of trust between pets and humans is often broken. Many people mistreat animals, either out of anger or ignorance. But the most common kind of animal abuse is neglect or abandonment.

Many people who buy puppies or kittens grow bored when the animals are no longer "cute." Some pet owners don't take the time to train their pets properly, and then blame the animal for not being housebroken. Unwanted pets are often turned loose on the streets. As a result, animal shelters are filled with millions of unwanted pets.

These unhappy cats are being kept at an animal shelter in Houston.

Most of these homeless animals are put to death a few weeks or months after they arrive. Exotic pets are even more likely to die this way than dogs or cats because they are more difficult to train and keep.

SPOILING OUR PETS

At the opposite extreme are people who indulge their pets too much. Many people lavish luxuries on their pets. Some pet boutiques even sell custom-made water beds, gold-plated choke chains, canine nail polish, and personalized, leather-covered dining suits. Dog clothing also includes raincoats, pullovers, frilly dresses, and underwear. Many pets are elegantly groomed at salons, have birthday parties, or go on vacations to hotels that cater to animals. Some pets even go to summer camp! A camp for dogs in upstate New York offers "spacious accommodations and a program of recreation for your canine camper." Each dog enjoys its own private cabin with 400 sq. feet (37 sq. m) of romping space, choice of meal plan, and lots of activities, including fetch, catch, and swimming.

When our pets get sick, they receive medical care that includes expensive tests and treatments as well as major operations. A few animals have even had pacemakers implanted to steady their heart beat.

Some people become so attached to their pets that they make provisions for them in their will. Occasionally, newspaper articles tell us about pets that have inherited

On Santa's Lap

A pet store in Ridgewood, New Jersey, recently offered customers an opportunity to have their pets photographed on Santa's lap. The animals who cuddled up on Santa's lap included poodles, dobermans, parakeets, rabbits, cats, and even a miniature potbellied pig.

Happy Birthday!

FINAL RESTING PLACE

When a pet dies, its owners may bury the animal in a pet cemetery. The graves are often marked with expensive headstones.

"The Pet Haven" in Gardena, California, contains the remains of more than 28,000 animals—including the favorite dogs of Hollywood celebrities. For a price, the owner is provided with a cemetery plot, a flower container, the services of a "groomer" to prepare the body for burial, and a viewing room where the owner can hold services.

In 1920, a shoemaker living in Newark, New Jersey, held an extravagant funeral for his pet canary. The ceremony, which more than 10,000 people attended, included a 15-piece band, a hearse and two coaches, and a fine white casket.

fortunes. One woman left her canary $250,000. When that bird died, the money was inherited by another canary named Co-Co and a cat named Tommie.

When American oil heiress Miss Eleanor Ritchey died in 1968, she left $4.5 million to the 150 stray dogs she kept on her ranch in Fort Lauderdale, Florida. The dogs lived in luxury and were cared for by a personal veterinarian and a ranch manager. When the last of the "heirs" died in 1984, the remaining money was given to a research foundation that studies animal diseases.

According to *The Guinness Book of Pet Records*, the world's richest cat was a white alley cat named Charlie Chan. Its owner—Mrs. Grace Alma Patterson of Joplin,

A pet cemetery in San Francisco, California

Missouri—left everything she owned to her 18-pound (8-kg) pet. The cat's inheritance included a three-bedroom house, a 7-acre (2.8-hectare) pet cemetery, and a collection of valuable antiques.

The Peaceable Kingdom was painted by Edward Hicks in 1847.

THE DREAM OF HARMONY

The human-animal bond is an amazing phenomenon. For centuries, people have dreamed of living in harmony with animals. The perfect example of this ideal is *The Peaceable Kingdom*, a painting by Edward Hicks that shows a person surrounded by friendly, gentle creatures, including a lion. Keeping animals as pets lets a little bit of that dream come true.

54

GLOSSARY

breed   To pick specific animals to mate and have young in order to create an animal with a particular appearance or behavior.

cold blooded   Having a body temperature that changes with the temperature of the animal's surroundings.

domestication   The act of training or changing a wild animal so that it can be used by people.

endangered   Threatened with extinction.

exotic   Special or unusual.

gape   The gesture a baby bird makes when it wants to be fed. The bird lifts its head and open its mouth wide for food.

gene   The material inside a cell that determines the traits that living things inherit from their parents.

inherit   To receive property from a dead relative; to receive genetic traits from a parent

mammal   A member of a group of animals that has a backbone and feeds its young with mother's milk.

metamorphosis   The process by which some young animals, especially insects, become adults.

prey   An animal that is hunted and killed for food.

rabies   A disease that affects the nervous system of mammals. Symptoms include abnormal behavior. It often causes paralysis and even death.

reptile   A member of a group of animals that lives on land, lays eggs, and is cold-blooded. Examples include alligators, turtles, snakes, and lizards.

species   A group of living things that have certain characteristics in common. Members of a species can mate and produce healthy young.

tame   To make a wild animal behave in a way that is beneficial to humans.

vivarium   A tank that contains both land and water areas.

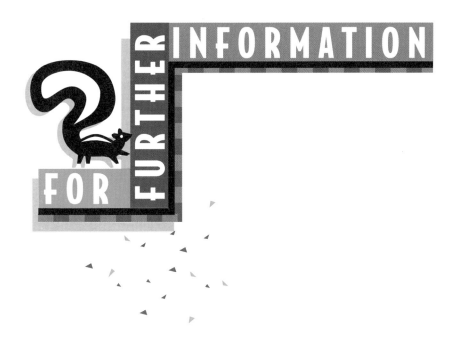

BOOKS FOR YOUNG READERS

Caulkins, Janet V. *Pets of the Presidents*. Brookfield, CT: Mill-
    brook Press, 1992.

George, Jean Craighead. *The Tarantula in My Purse*. New
    York: HarperCollins, 1996.

Hess, Lilo. *Problem Pets*. New York: Charles Scribner's Sons,
    1972.

Kellner, Esther. *Animals Come to My House*. New York: G.P.
    Putnam's Sons, 1976.

Piecewicz, Ann Thomas. *See What I Caught*. Englewood Cliffs,
    NJ: Prentice Hall, 1974.

Rood, Ronald. *May I Keep this Clam, Mother? It Followed Me Home. The Care & Feeding of Wild Pets.* New York: Simon and Schuster, 1973.

Sprackland, Robert G. Jr. *All About Lizards.* Neptune City, NJ: T.F.H. Publications, 1977.

Storer, Pat. *Pot Bellies and other Miniature Pigs.* Happauge, NY: Barron's, 1992.

Squire, Ann. *101 Questions & Answers About Backyard Wildlife.* New York: Walker & Co., 1996.

Weber, William J. *Wild Orphan Friends.* New York: Holt, Rinehart and Winston, 1976.

Vandivert, Rita. *Understanding Animals as Pets.* New York: Frederick Warne & Co., 1975.

Zeaman, John. *Climbing onto the Horse's Back.* Danbury, CT: Franklin Watts, 1997.

_____. *How the Wolf Became the Dog.* Danbury, CT: Franklin Watts, 1997.

_____. *Why the Cats Chose Us.* Danbury, CT: Franklin Watts, 1997.

FOR ADVANCED READERS

Beck, Alan and Aaron Katcher. *Between Pets and People: The Importance of Animal Companionship.* New York: G.P. Putnam's Sons, 1983.

Burn, Barbara. *A Practical Guide to Impractical Pets.* New York: Howell Book House, 1997.

Clutton-Brock, Juliet. *A Natural History of Domesticated Animals.* Austin, TX: University of Texas Press, 1989.

Cooper, Gale. *Animal People.* Boston: Houghton Mifflin, 1983.

Mattison, Chris. *A Practical Guide to Exotic Pets*. Philadelphia, PA: Running Press, 1994.

Rosenfeld, Arthur. *Exotic Pets*. New York: Simon & Schuster, 1987.

Serpell, James. *In the Company of Animals: A History of Human-Animal Relationships*. New York: B. Blackwell, 1986.

Szasz, Kathleen. *Petishism, Pets and their People in the Western World*. New York: Holt, Rinehart and Winston, 1968.

INTERNET SITES

http://www.aspca.org/

This is the home page of the American Society for the Prevention of Cruelty to Animals (ASPCA), an organization dedicated to the prevention of cruelty to animals.

http://www.batnet.com/wildlife/

Wildlife Rescue is an organization dedicated to rehabilitating and releasing local wildlife and to providing an educational forum for wildlife-related issues.

http://www.teleport.com/~cos/noah/

This is the home page for NOAH's Exotic, a federal and state licensed non-profit corporation that helps wild and endangered animals. The group provides food, shelter, and medical care for animals in need and educates the public about the animals and how to care for them. This organization doesn't have e-mail, but you can write to them at W. 5035 Highway 53, Rathdrum, ID 83858.

http://www.petpeople.com/

Do you need a name for a pet? Would you like to read some funny pet stories? Would you like to communicate with other pet owners? This is the site for you. There's even a special section just for kids.

http://www.thepetchannel.com/
This site provides resources for pet owners.

http://www.voicenet.com/-johnpac/bacon.html
If you love potbellied pigs, check out this site. It has information about products and organizations for pot-bellied pigs and their owners as well as frequently asked questions about potbellied pigs.

INDEX

Page numbers in *italics* indicate illustrations.

61

ABOUT THE AUTHOR

John Zeaman is a journalist. For the past 13 years, he has been a critic, feature writer, and editor with the *Bergen Record* of New Jersey. His interest in pets and animal domestication stems from the numerous pets that have lived in his household, including a standard poodle, two cats, gerbils, a parakeet, finches, lizards, turtles, a garter snake, and, briefly, a wild squirrel. The idea for this series grew out of a project that his daughter did in the fifth grade on the origins of pets. He lives in Leonia, New Jersey, with his wife, Janet, and their children, Claire and Alex.